Must God Punish Sin?

Ben Cooper

The Latimer Trust

Must God Punish Sin?

© by Ben Cooper 2006
ISBN 0-946307-55-5
EAN 978-0-946307-55-5

Published by the Latimer Trust
PO Box 26685
London N14 4XQ

www.latimertrust.org

CONTENTS

1.   Introduction

Must God punish sin?

What do we mean by that question? That the God who
engages with his people through the Bible describes himself
as a punishing God seems clear from the Scriptures, as we
shall see more fully in Section 2, but of course the idea is
hugely controversial. Is divine punishment disciplinary,
aimed at changing behaviour? Or is it 'retributive'? (And what
do we mean by 'retributive'?) These are some of the questions
we shall seek to address in the course of this study.

But to ask whether it is *necessary* for God to punish sin
introduces a whole new level of discussion. What does it
mean to say that something like punishing sin is 'necessary'?
Roughly speaking, we may say that 'necessity' refers to that
which could not have been otherwise. So if we say that divine
punishment of sin is necessary, we are saying that there is no
way that God could not do it.[1]

Historically, the question of whether it is necessary for God to
punish sin has received very little extended attention in recent
centuries. We may look to Faustus Socinus[2] for the seminal
argument, in 1594, that it is *not* necessary for God to punish
sin: that he may choose not to punish sin without
satisfaction. The opposite view, that it is absolutely necessary
that God punish sin, receives its most complete expression in
John Owen's *Dissertation on Divine Justice* (1653).[3] We shall

---

[1] We shall briefly clarify this at the beginning of Section 3.
[2] In F. Socinus, *De Jesu Christo Servatore*, 1594, in *Fausti Socinin Opera*, vol.1
(Irenopoli, 1656).
[3] J. Owen, *A Dissertation on Divine Justice*, hereafter *DDJ* (Oxford, Thomas
Robinson, 1653), in W. H. Goold (ed.) *The Works of John Owen*, vol. 10 (London,

be interacting with Socinus and Owen at length below. But there is relatively little to engage with since the seventeenth century.

However, the relative lack of attention given to this issue in recent times is in sharp contrast to its doctrinal importance. Moreover, since good pastoral practice always depends on sound doctrine, the pastoral implications are significant too. This is much more than some abstract debate on what is, and what is not, 'essential' to God. The question obviously has direct implications for the doctrine of salvation: striking right at the heart of what it means when we proclaim the command to repent and believe the gospel.

We see this in Socinus himself. Part of Socinus' argument that it is God's right not to punish sin is to present God as a creditor with the absolute right to cancel the debt of our sin without receiving satisfaction. There was therefore no need for Christ by his death to make satisfaction for our sins to God. By rejecting the necessity of divine punishment, Socinus is drawn to a non-penal doctrine of the atonement in which sinners are saved by imitating the way of salvation revealed by Christ.

We also see it in many contemporary treatments of the doctrine of salvation. Not only is an automatic relation between sin and punishment seen as 'mechanistic' and 'impersonal',[4] modern writers such as Paul Fiddes go beyond Socinus by breaking the link between God's anger at sin and

---

Johnstone & Hunter, 1850-55), pp.481-624.
[4] See G. Williams, 'The Cross and the Punishment of Sin', in D. Peterson (ed.), *Where Wrath and Mercy Meet: Proclaiming the Atonement Today*, (Carlisle, Paternoster, 2001), pp.81-4.

the exercise of vindicatory punishment altogether (for even Socinus would be happy to insist that God will punish the unrepentant). For Fiddes, God 'passes his verdict against sinful human life in order to awaken a spirit of penitence'.[5] Jesus' humility on the cross then becomes an example and an act of solidarity for those disobedient children who wish to return to the bosom of their Father.

To take another example, evangelicals in Anglican circles need to be aware of the Doctrine Commission's 1995 report on *The Mystery of Salvation*.[6] The writers of the report rightly recognise in the first chapter that 'if we are to speak of salvation in a Christian sense we also have to seek more clarity about the peril in which the world is believed to stand'.[7] However, they openly wonder whether the traditional Christian description of the peril as 'the power of sin and its consequence, death' can be deemed meaningful in a secular society.[8] And it is not at all obvious that they come to any clear conclusions as to what a meaningful description of the peril might be – not surprising, then, that salvation seems to remain for them something of a 'mystery'. They certainly do not describe the peril in which the world stands as being under a sentence of divine punishment. Indeed, the doctrine of atonement expressed in the 39 Articles is dismissed as excessively 'juridicial': an over-emphasis on legal categories

---

[5] P. Fiddes, *Past Event and Present Salvation* (London; Darton, Longman & Todd, 1989), p.105ff.
[6] The Mystery of Salvation: The Story of God's Gift, a Report by the Doctrine Commission of the General Synod of the Church of England (London, Church House Publishing, 1995).
[7] Ibid., p.1.
[8] Ibid., pp.2-27.

over moral ones.[9]

And even within ostensibly evangelical circles strong doubts have recently been raised about whether it is valid to talk about God as a punishing God. Steve Chalke argues that the rhetoric of judgement and punishment in Christian teaching has masked the fact that God defines himself as love (1 John 4:8), a truth that has become 'one of the world's best-kept secrets'.[10] Indeed, Chalke goes so far as to say that 'the Bible never defines God as anger, power or judgment – in fact it never defines him as anything other than love'. So that 'however else God may have revealed himself, and in whatever way he interacts with the world he has created, everything is to be tempered, interpreted, understood and seen through the one primary lens of God's love'.[11] And, again, it is not surprising to see this re-emphasis resulting in a non-penal doctrine of the atonement. According to Chalke, the death and resurrection of Jesus 'prove that he was telling the truth so that we can trust him'.[12] His suffering 'absorbed all the pain, all the suffering caused by the breakdown in our relationship with God and in doing so he demonstrated the lengths to which a God who is love will go to restore it'.[13] In his cry of dereliction Jesus was identifying with 'the countless millions of people who suffer oppression, enslavement, abuse, disease, poverty, starvation and violence'.[14] The doctrine that Jesus might be bearing punishment on the

---

[9] Ibid., pp.207-215.
[10] S. Chalke, and A. Mann, *The Lost Message of Jesus* (Grand Rapids, Zondervan, 2004), p.55.
[11] Ibid., p.63.
[12] Ibid., p.173.
[13] Ibid., p.181
[14] Ibid., p.184.

cross is dismissed as 'a form of cosmic child abuse'.[15]

Uncertainty concerning the nature and purpose of punishment seems to lie at the heart of the rejection of penal doctrine throughout church history and especially today. Does such uncertainty have any biblical warrant? In this study we shall attempt to examine the *foundations* of the orthodox doctrine of the atonement, as found in the doctrine of divine punishment. If the determination to punish sin is not part of the divine will, then non-penal doctrines of the atonement start to look more credible. On the other hand, if the relation between sin and the exercise of divine punishment is very close, then this would seem to imply that the atonement *has* to involve a penal element. So the question is this: must God punish sin?

That is the question tackled at a popular level in my book *Just Love: Why God Must Punish Sin.*[16] The aim of this paper is to tackle the same issue by engaging with the biblical material and the historic debate in a deeper and broader manner. Section 2 presents an overview of the biblical data on divine punishment. In Section 3, we shall then investigate which lines of argument concerning divine punishment are consistent with the biblical material, engaging with, amongst others, Socinus, Owen, Edwards and Turretin.

The importance of the subject should already be apparent. This is an issue so close to the heart of what it means for God to be God, and so much at the centre of what it means for God to save his people, that, to use Jonathan Edward's

---

[15] Ibid., p.182.
[16] B. Cooper, *Just Love: why God must punish sin* (New Malden, The Good Book Company, 2005).

memorable phrase, it simply 'is of such importance as to *demand* attention'.[17] Its application is found in what we preach and teach concerning the character of God and concerning his gospel of salvation. And my aim in writing a more technical account has been to encourage multiple popular presentations of the doctrine of divine punishment from *many* pastors and teachers ministering in *many* situations. Nevertheless, there are also a number of other particular lines of application we can pursue, and these will be highlighted in the conclusion.

---

[17] J. Edwards, *Freedom of the Will,* edited by P. Ramsey, (New Haven and London, Yale University Press, 1957; first published 1754), p.133.

2. The Biblical Data on Divine Punishment Against a Contemporary Backdrop

We begin with an all-too-brief survey of the biblical data on divine punishment. The aim is to summarise some of the main themes in the description of divine punishment and to make some preliminary observations regarding its purpose, in a fashion that will prove helpful when it comes to constructing and assessing the more systematic arguments about divine punishment in Section 3. However, we need to be aware that the discussion of divine punishment takes place within a specific cultural context. It will therefore be helpful to see this data against the backdrop of alternative contemporary understandings of the concept of punishment.

2.1. The Secular Understanding of 'Punishment'

2.1.1. Defining 'punishment'

Dictionary definitions of 'punishment'[18] tend to include three elements:

(P1)   The imposition of a state of affairs on an offender they would prefer not to experience;

(P2)   in response to a particular offence, or set of offences;

(P3)   administered by a legitimate authority.

---

[18] e.g. O. O'Donovan and R. J. Song, 'Punishment' in the *New Dictionary of Theology*, ed. S. B. Ferguson and D. F. Wright (Leicester, IVP, 1988), pp.547-549.

However, the dominant contemporary understanding of punishment, which sees it as no more than one component of the way people interact socially, actually works under a much weaker definition. Given contemporary antipathy to 'authority' as a primitive concept, it is not surprising to find (P3) dropping out, giving (at least implicitly) the weaker definition:

(P1)   (as above);

(P2)′   in response to a deviation from a norm.

2.1.2.   *The behavioural model of punishment*

The 'socially descriptive' view of punishment implied by this weaker definition finds its most developed and precise expression in the theory of repeated games,[19] where 'punishment' is that part of an individual's pattern of behaviour (or 'strategy') intended to influence credibly the behaviour of others. For example, in this literature, social interaction is often (to an over-stretched degree[20]) modelled as a 'repeated prisoners' dilemma', in which individuals have a choice about whether to act cooperatively or not in social

---

[19] Which in more precise terminologies are termed 'supergames' to distinguish them from more general dynamic games. See J.-F. Mertens, 'Supergames', in *The New Palgrave: Game Theory*, edited by J. Eatwell, M. Milgate and P. Newman (London, Macmillan, 1987), pp.238-241; M. J. Osborne and A. Rubinstein, *A Course in Game Theory*, (Cambridge, Mass.; MIT Press, 1994), pp.133-162; D. Fudenberg and J. Tirole, *Game Theory*, (Cambridge, Mass; MIT Press, 1991), pp.145-206; K. Binmore, *Game Theory and the Social Contract*. Volume I, *Playing Fair*, (Cambridge MA, MIT Press, 1994), pp.115-117; Volume II, *Just Playing*, (Cambridge MA, MIT Press, 1998), pp.293-328.
[20] A popular example being its central place in R. Axelrod, *The Evolution of Cooperation*, (Harmondsworth, Penguin Books, 1990).

situations.[21] In the repeated prisoners' dilemma, people do better on average in societies in which everyone cooperates, but there is a short-run incentive for people to 'cheat' and exploit the good-will of their neighbours. But the norm of cooperation can be maintained if people adopt strategies that involve 'punishing' a deviation from cooperation by responding in kind. In equilibrium (i.e. if everyone chooses the strategy that is best for them, given everyone else's choices), under perfect information about what is going on, the threat of punishment is credible and the behavioural norm is maintained.[22]

It is possible to expand this approach to encompass the institutional administration of punishment.[23] This gives us an explanation of how the legitimacy of a given authority is established: it is purely by social convention.

While most contemporary writers on punishment would not use the language of repeated games, there is a common emphasis on the purpose of punishment being to influence behaviour. It appears to be a very general approach; it encompasses the theories of 'deterrence' and 'rehabilitation',[24] and lends itself well to popular

---

[21] Strictly speaking, it is not necessary to be so specific about the exact nature of the social interaction, but focussing on the repeated prisoners' dilemma will serve to show what 'punishment' actually looks like under this way of thinking.

[22] However, punishment need not be hypothetical if people make mistakes when monitoring others' behaviour.

[23] Binmore, *Game Theory and the Social Contract*, Volume II, *op. cit.*, pp.271-2, 328-339.

[24] O. O'Donovan and R. J. Song, *op. cit.*. It is not being too cynical to see 'rehabilitation' as one way of accentuating the effect of punishment in the future. The more bourgeois one can make an offender through education, the greater the cost of social ostracism should they be caught re-offending.

consequentialist assessments of the social norms that punishment supports.

So far, of course, we have made no reference to God. Were one to include him, then we might be led to some sort of crude 'Governmental' theory, in which divine punishment only functions to serve the future good of society as a whole by providing a deterrent against sin.[25] In this view, the cross would then be *no more* than a particularly graphic example of what God will do to sinners.

2.1.3. *Allowing for retribution*

As a descriptive model that captures some features of the way societies function, the behavioural model may have some merit. However, the apparent generality of the behavioural view is deceptive. The framework rules out by assumption any understanding in which punishment has a purpose *apart* from influencing behaviour. We shall want at least to allow for the possibility of this being a characteristic of the biblical data on divinely administered punishment, so we must be careful not to be constrained by the behavioural view.

That is, we shall want to allow for the possibility of divine punishment that has a *retributive* aspect, where we shall work with the following definition:

(R)   The retributive element of punishment is that *aspect*

---

[25] Garry Williams argues strongly that the governmental theory expressed by Hugo Grotius is not so crude as this. As we shall note below, punishment (including that taken by Jesus on the cross) can have behavioural effects while remaining fundamentally retributive. See G. J. Williams, *A Critical Exposition of Hugo Grotius's Doctrine of the Atonement in* De satisfactione Christi, unpublished D.Phil. thesis (Oxford, 1999), pp.132-139.

of an act of punishment that is not intended to have any effect on behaviour.

Two comments are worth making before proceeding. The first is that to describe punishment as 'retributive' does not exclude the possibility that it might also have a behavioural element. For example, one can argue that many New Testament warnings of punishment function to keep the elect persevering, but that the punishment they threaten is still retributive.[26] The purpose of punishment that is *purely* retributive is such that it is exercised even if it, or the threat of its use, were to have no behavioural effects.

Secondly, in this definition we have only said what the purpose of the retributive element of punishment is *not.* In particular, we have said nothing yet about its purpose that warrants the label 'impersonal' or 'mechanical', or that ties it to a particular 'transactional' model of punishment.[27]

2.2. The Biblical Data on Divine Punishment

The biblical presentation of divine punishment is multi-faceted. We may find, for example, *warnings* of punishment, sometimes with conditions attached. Associated with this, there may be statements about God's character related to the giving of the warning. Then there may be a description of the sentence and actual exercise of punishment. This may involve some withholding or mitigation of the punishment promised. Finally, there may be a direct statement of purpose linked to

---

[26] Indeed, one might add that it is the retributive nature of the threatened punishment that makes the warnings credible.
[27] Such as that often attributed to Anselm of Canterbury — see discussion in Section 3.2.2.

the exercise of the punishment.

Consider the paradigmatic divine punishment described in Gen. 1-4. There is a clear warning in Gen. 2:17 that emphasises the inevitability of death in the event of a particular sin. The sin takes place (3:1-7) and sentence of punishment follows (3:16-19).[28] However, the actual exercise of the death sentence does not appear to happen straightforwardly. On the one hand, we need to note the language that suggests 'the Garden of Eden is a temple-garden, represented later in the tabernacle'.[29] Cherubim guard its sanctity (compare 3:24 with Exod. 26:1 and 2 Chron. 3:7). So the expulsion of 3:21-24 may be compared to expulsion from the camp of Israel.[30] Outside the camp was a forsaken place (Lev 24:14-23; Num 5:3-4, 15:35-36) where one often required purification before re-entry.[31] We may usefully label this immediate aspect of the punishment, the relational separation from the source of life, as 'spiritual' death. On the other hand, physical death, although now inevitable (Gen. 3:19), does not happen immediately. Once driven from the place of blessing (3:22-24), the first physical death is not directly administered by God at all but at the hands of the

---

[28] In the light of 3:19, it is extraordinary that Krašovek should claim that both 'the fall of Adam and Eve is not something that deserves death' (J. Krašovek, *Reward, Punishment and Forgiveness: The Thinking and Beliefs of Ancient Israel in the Light of Greek and Modern Views*, VT sup. 78 (Leiden, Brill, 1999), p.28) and that the sentence of 3:17-19 is 'severe but not catastrophic' (Ibid., p.29). As Wenham notes, in 3:17 the sentence is introduced as an enactment of the warning in 2:17, and although there is delay (3:17b-18), 'the original threat is endorsed' in v.19 (G. J. Wenham, *Genesis 1-15*, WBC (Waco, Texas; Word Books, 1987), p.83).
[29] B. K. Waltke, *Genesis: A Commentary*, (Grand-Rapids, Michigan; Zondervan, 2001), p.85.
[30] Wenham, *op. cit.*, p.90.
[31] Lev 10:4, 14:3-32, 16:28; Num 19:9-10, 31:19-20; Deut 23:10-11

murderer Cain (4:8). Adam's physical death is over 800 years later (5:5).

There is no *direct* statement of purpose attached to this particular exercise of divine punishment. In fact, direct statements of purpose attached to the exercise of divine punishment are actually rather rare. More common is to have some statement concerning God's character associated with the issue of a warning or advance notice of punishment. This can take many forms. For example, when God reveals to Abraham the punishment he is about to exercise on Sodom and Gomorrah in Gen. 18:16-33, the statement concerning God's status and character comes as part of the dialogue. Abraham asks the rhetorical question, 'Shall not the judge of all the earth do what is just?' (18:25).

There is obviously not the space here to consider every biblical reference to divine punishment — valuable though such an exercise would be. One, albeit rather limited, way of getting some insight into the material as a whole is to consider the vocabulary of divine punishment, and we shall consider this briefly in the next section. We shall then consider three major examples of divine punishment: at the Exodus, in the destruction of Jerusalem, and at the future eschatological 'day of the LORD'. These have been chosen because of the way they span the different ways of describing divine punishment, and for their importance in salvation history.

2.2.1. *Lexical Analysis*

James Barr's seminal work on *The Semantics of Biblical*

Language, and especially his critique of the linguistic method of the ten-volume *Theological Dictionary of the New Testament*,[32] has introduced a healthy caution against over-relying on word-studies as a source of theological insight. However, the biblical authors *do* make theologically significant choices of vocabulary and patterns of word usage, and there are a number of important points to be learned from the vocabulary of divine punishment.

2.2.1.1. The relation between anger and punishment

The first point we can make is that there is a close association between words describing divine punishment and words describing divine anger, and they often appear in the same context.

Bruce Baloian usefully notes that the motive clauses associated with divine wrath indicate that it is provoked by human interpersonal wickedness in some 25% of cases, direct rebellion against Yahweh's person in some 42% of cases, and some combination of the two in the remainder[33] (and they are of course closely related). That expressions of anger are accompanied by such motive clauses 'evidence rationality' in Yahweh's reaction: it is neither 'capricious nor unpredictable'. Indeed, 'if there is unpredictability in Yahweh, it is in his extension of grace, not judgement'.[34] This is of course in contrast to the unreasonable passions of the

---

[32] J. Barr, *The Semantics of Biblical Language* (Oxford, OUP, 1961), pp.206-287.
[33] B. Baloian, 'Anger', in W. A. VanGemeren (ed.), *New International Dictionary of Old Testament Theology and Exegesis* (hereafter *NIDOTTE*), 5 vols. (Carlise, Paternoster, 1997), vol.4, p.381.
[34] Ibid., p.382.

Ancient Near Eastern deities.[35]

The important point to make is that this judgement is not merely expressed verbally. Baloian notes that only four cases where Yahweh's anger is proclaimed fail to mention him acting upon it in the immediate context: 'when he is angry, this is tangibly experienced in the world'.[36] There is a striking example in Ps. 78:49-50 where, commenting on the punishment of Egypt (see Section 2.2.2 below), the author says God 'made level a pathway' for his anger.

The relationship seems especially close in those words for anger with connotations of fire or burning. Many of the Hebrew words for anger include heat, burning or fire in their semantic range; the proximity of the words used in the sense of anger with graphic fire-imagery suggests that they have not lost this connotation. The connotation of burning might simply indicate 'the inward fire of the emotion of anger',[37] but the usage of these words suggests otherwise. In Jer. 4:4, for example, the threat is that the 'burning anger' (ḥēmâh) of the LORD will *go forth* like fire, and not be quenched.

2.2.1.2. *The relation between sin and punishment*

The second lexical point to make is the overlap between the semantic fields of iniquity, sin and guilt on the one hand, and punishment on the other. So words more commonly associated with iniquity, sin and guilt —such as ʿāōn, ḥēṭ ᵉʾ and ḥaṭṭâʾt — are sometimes used as metonyms for

---

[35] G. Herion, 'Wrath of God (OT)', *Anchor Bible Dictionary*, vol. 6 (New York, Doubleday, 1992), pp.991-992.
[36] Baloian, *op. cit.*, p.382.
[37] W. Eichrodt, *Theology of the Old Testament*, vol. 1 (London, SCM, 1961), p.258.

punishment. That an author chooses a 'sin' word to denote punishment does suggest some close theological association between the two in his mind. Of course, the association could be no more than that in some way sin is its own punishment — as Luc expresses the idea, 'punishment is inherent in sin'.[38] There is no doubt some truth in this (e.g. Prov. 5:22), although it certainly does not exclude God's hand in the punishment (Rom. 1:18ff). Moreover, the words are often used of direct divine punishment. An important example is the punishment of Sodom in Gen. 19:15: ʿāōn, used of sin in 15:16 and 44:16, is here used of that which will consume the city in sulphur and fire (19:24).

Similarly, in his investigation of the language of 'sin-bearing' in Isa. 53:11, Garry Williams notes how often sin-bearing language is used to indicate the bearing of punishment.[39] For example, bearing ʿāōn most likely refers to the punishment just inflicted on Cain in Gen. 4:13, and most certainly refers to punishment in Num. 14:34 and Lam. 5:7. Bearing ḥēṭ ʿ in Lev. 24:15 refers to the stoning of a blasphemer. Moreover, 'even where the sense is limited to guilt-bearing, the notion of following punishment is never far away'.[40]

A related point is the close contextual association of 'sin' words and words denoting death. Luc notes that ḥēṭ ʿ and 'death' occur in the same context or vicinity over 60 times in the Hebrew Scriptures.[41]

---

[38] A. Luc, 'חטא', *NIDOTTE* vol.2, p.90.
[39] G. J. Williams, 'The Cross and the Punishment of Sin', *op. cit.*, pp.70-75.
[40] Ibid., p.72.
[41] Luc, *op. cit.*, p.89.

2.2.1.3. *The distinction between chastisement and vengeance*

A third point is that the vocabulary of divine punishment is able to make a clear distinction between the behavioural notion of 'chastisement' on the one hand, and the non-behavioural notion of 'vengeance' on the other.

There are distinct words for chastisement, correction or discipline in *yāsar*, *mûsār* and the corresponding Greek words *paideuō* and *paideia* (compare Prov. 3:11-12 to Heb. 12:5-6). This does not mean that other words for punishment cannot carry these connotations. However, discipline is held as something distinct from the expression of God's anger in, for example, Jer. 10:24.

In contrast, the biblical evidence makes it very difficult to sustain the thesis that 'God's vengeance is usually disciplinary in nature'[42] — at least at the level of individuals experiencing that vengeance. Indeed, in *none* of the instances of the verb *nāqam* ('avenge'; cf. the Greek verb *ekdikeō* — Rom. 12:19; Rev. 6:10 etc.) is there any suggestion of changed behaviour — either on the part of those experiencing God's vengeance, or on those witnessing it. In Isa. 1:24, for example, the expression of vengeance against God's enemies is followed by the restoration of Zion in v.26. However, there is no suggestion that his enemies repent; rather, they are simply removed from the scene like 'dross' (v.25). Similarly in Nahum, where the Lord is described as 'jealous and avenging' (Nah. 1:2), and this means he will 'by no means' (infinitive absolute with the imperfect) clear the guilty (v.3). One may perhaps talk about vengeance being disciplinary for

---

[42] H. G. L. Peels, 'נקם', *NIDOTTE* vol. 3, p.155.

Israel 'personified', as a way of talking about the purification of Zion taken as a whole — but that is a rather different idea.

2.2.2. *The Egyptian Plagues*

The punishment of Egypt associated with the Exodus gives a paradigmatic example of punishment in its relation to redemption.

God's instruction to Moses in Exod. 7:2-5 gives a useful summary of the plague narrative that follows (7:8-10:29). We find that the plagues take place in the context of Moses and Aaron passing on the command of God to Pharaoh to let his people go (7:2; cf. 5:1; 7:16; 8:1, 20; 9:1, 13; 10:3); and these are accompanied by warnings of the consequences of disobedience in 8:2, 21; 9:2-3, 14-19 and 10:1-6. The 'signs and wonders' (7:3) are punishments of increasing intensity; they are increasingly difficult to imitate, and increasingly directed at the Egyptians as distinct from the Israelites in their effect.[43] They culminate in the striking down of the firstborn of Egypt (12:29-30), a 'great deed of vindicating judgement' (7:4).

The purpose of these punishments is clearly not straightforwardly behavioural. Although Pharaoh does relent after some of the plagues (8:8, 28; 9:27-28; 10:16-17, 24; 12:31), and this does result in the (temporary) withholding of punishment, the change of heart is in each case short-lived. The plagues take place in the context of God's foreknowledge of Pharaoh's disobedience (7:4); indeed, we cannot escape the fact that God is throughout actively involved in hardening his

---

[43] See the very useful table in P. Enns, *Exodus*, NIV Application Commentary (Grand Rapids, Michigan; Zondervan, 2000), p.194.

heart (7:3; also 4:21; 9:12; 10:1, 20, 27; 11:10; 14:4, 8, 17).

The primary purpose is rather expressed in the recognition formula: 'And so the Egyptians shall know that I am the LORD' (7:5; cf. 7:17; 14:4, 18); and, indeed, that the LORD is in Egypt (8:22). It is to show that there is no one like the LORD (8:10; 9:14). He lets Pharaoh live as witness to his power; he does it 'to make my name be related' in all the earth (9:15-16). The punishments demonstrate to Pharaoh that the earth is the LORD's (9:29). They also demonstrate to the Israelites that the LORD is their God (6:7; 10:1-2). The final climatic striking down of the firstborn of Egypt is described as executing judgements on all the gods of Egypt (12:12). Again, the declaration is 'I am the LORD'.

We shall make two further observations:

The first concerns the recognition formulae. Walter Zimmerli's seminal work on the biblical recognition formulae[44] is perhaps more concerned than we are here with form-critical issues.[45] Nevertheless, his account is helpful in emphasizing both the pervasiveness of the recognition formulae in Scripture (not just in the Exodus account and in Ezekiel, but also in 1 Kings, the Psalms, Isaiah, Jeremiah and Joel,[46] with similar structures found elsewhere) and their *theological* importance. Zimmerli sees the recognition formulae as the fusion of two ideas. The first is the idea of a

---

[44] W. Zimmerli, 'I am Yahweh' (first published 1954), reprinted in W. Zimmerli, *I am Yahweh*, trans. D. W. Stott (Atlanta, John Knox Press, 1982), pp.1-28; 'Knowledge of God According to the Book of Ezekiel' (first published 1954), reprinted in Zimmerli, *I am Yahweh*, pp.29-98.
[45] Zimmerli, 'Knowledge of God According to the Book of Ezekiel', p.63.
[46] e.g. 1 Kings 20:28; Psalm 46:10; Isaiah 41:17-20, 45:2-3; Jeremiah 24:7; Joel 2:27.

proof-sign:[47] an act which brings about the recognition or acknowledgement of some truth. Indeed, the *purpose* and *goal* of the act is such acknowledgement.[48] The role of the prophet in this is to draw attention to the act, such that the purpose and goal of the prophetic proclamation is also such acknowledgement.[49] The second idea is the self-introduction expressed in the phrase 'I am Yahweh' – a statement 'laden with significance and basically self-contained'.[50] This is the truth which the recognition formulae declare will be acknowledged by those who witness, experience or hear the prophetic word about a given act: 'from his works one can recognize that Yahweh is king, that he is the holy judge, indeed, that he is God'.[51]

What Zimmerli does not do is link the statement 'I am Yahweh' to all the references to the disclosure of God's name in the book of Exodus. He does note that in Exodus 6:2-8 (cf. Ezek. 20:5-7) 'I am Yahweh' introduces Yahweh as the name of the covenant LORD fulfilling his promises to the patriarchs.[52] However, the significance of the LORD making 'his name known in all the earth' (9:16) is better understood when we read on to 34:6-7. We already know that the LORD's name is associated with his self-sufficiency (3:14). In 34:6-7 we learn that it represents his mercy, slowness to anger, faithful love and forgiveness of sin; yet it also represents the fact that he will 'by no means' (infinitive absolute with the

---

[47] Zimmerli, 'Knowledge of God According to the Book of Ezekiel', p.79.
[48] Ibid., p.50.
[49] Ibid., pp.37, 60, 68.
[50] Zimmerli, 'I am Yahweh', p.19.
[51] Zimmerli, 'Knowledge of God According to the Book of Ezekiel', p.83.
[52] Zimmerli, 'I am Yahweh', pp.7-8.

imperfect) leave sin (or 'the guilty') unpunished[53] (34:7; cf. Num. 14:18[54]). All of these characteristics are demonstrated in the plague narrative, but in particular we may note that had the LORD failed to punish Pharaoh's rebellion, then he would have failed to make his name known.

The second observation is related. This concerns punishment in relation to redemption; that is, how punishment is *avoided* in the plague narrative. It is true that the Israelites are not *explicitly* depicted as under threat of punishment within the plague narrative itself, but as the narrative later unfolds it becomes increasingly clear that they must have been. That is, it becomes clear how difficult it is for the LORD to accompany his people to the promised land without either compromising his holiness or destroying them in his wrath (33:3). If making his name known means not leaving the guilty unpunished, this implies special measures must have been needed to avoid punishment. So in the plague narrative, avoidance of the climatic punishment is exclusively for those Israelites who sprinkle their doorposts and lintels with the blood of a sacrifice (12:7). The blood proclaims a death[55] that averts the punishment of God (12:12-13, 23; cf. Heb. 11:28).

2.2.3.   *The Destruction of Jerusalem*

Even a cursory read through the Prophets shows the large quantity of biblical material dedicated to the punishment of Israel's apostasy, expressed in the Northern exile (2 Kings

---

[53] J. P. J. Olivier, 'נקה', *NIDOTTE*, vol. 3, pp.152-153.
[54] Also cf. Exod. 20:7; Job 9:28; Jer. 30:11; 46:28; Nah. 1:3.
[55] Since it is of course 'impossible for the blood of bulls and goats to take away sins' (Heb. 10:4), any actual aversion of God's judgment must have been made retrospectively through *Christ's* death (Heb. 9:15; cf. Rom. 3:25-26).

17:1-18), the subjection and exile of Judah (2 Kings 24:1-19; 2 Chr. 36:1-10), and culminating in the siege and destruction of Jerusalem (2 Kings 24:20-25:17; 2 Chr. 36:11-21; cf. Jer. 39:1-10; Ezek. 24:2; Lam. 1-2 and *passim*).

The depiction of divine punishment here has many parallels to that described against Egypt. The warnings of covenant curse from Moses and the prophets are sometimes accompanied by a command to repent (e.g. 'seek me and live' in Amos 5:4, 6); but, as with Pharaoh, there is no real expectation from the beginning that the warning will be heeded (Deut 29:4, 18-29; 32:26-29, 35). The warnings and exercise of this punishment cannot therefore legitimately be described as primarily behavioural in intent.

Again, *direct* purpose statements are relatively rare — except in Ezekiel, where they parallel the Exodus recognition formulae. Just as the Exodus punishments revealed the authority of the true God in a land of false gods, so the punishment of Jerusalem reveals the authority of the true God in the context of idolatry (e.g. Jer. 16:18-21; Ezek. 14:1-11) and false prophecy (e.g. Ezek. 13:1-16). But the exercise of punishment also reveals that it is by punishing people according to their ways (Ezek. 7:9, 27), and for the sake of his name (20:44), that Yahweh makes himself known.

However, the punishment warned of by the Prophets differs from that described in the Exodus account in the diversity of voices by which, and contexts in which, the warnings are given. The warnings also contain much more detail about their relation to the character of God in opposing sin. In Jeremiah, for example, God is doing far more than just asserting his authority in warning of punishment; rather, he is provoked to anger by the behaviour of his people (Jer. 7:18; 8:19; 11:17; 25:6-7; 32:29-32; 44:3, 8). He could no longer bear being confronted by their evil doings and abominations (44:22). The consequence is wrath like burning fire (7:20; 21:12), like a whirling tempest that will not cease until the LORD has executed the intent of his heart (23:19-20). As we also saw in the lexical study of Section 2.2.1, the structure of the warnings of the destruction of Jerusalem strongly suggests that punishment is merely the inevitable, practical exercise of God's hatred of sin.

2.2.4.   *The Day of Yahweh and the Day of Christ*

Van Leeuwen links the expression 'Day of Yahweh' back to 1 Sam. 26:10, where 'his day', when applied to Saul, is the 'day of his final destiny, on which the LORD will strike him down' (cf. Job 18:20; Ps 37:13; Ezek. 21:30; Obad. 12). The 'Day of Yahweh' is then the day by which Yahweh 'decrees and brings about the final destiny, the death of men'.[56]

As von Rad notes, 'the concepts connected with the Day of Yahweh are... in no way eschatological *per se*, but were familiar to the prophets in all their details'[57] — from events such as the punishment of Egypt and Jerusalem considered above, but also from the holy wars of occupation. So in Ezekiel and Lamentations the 'Day of Yahweh' refers to the fall of Jerusalem (Ezek. 7:19; 13:5; cf. 34:12; Lam. 2:21-22). It is possible, then, that announcements of the 'Day of Yahweh' for individual nations (Jer. 46:2-12 (Egypt); Ezek. 30:1-8 (Egypt); Isa. 13 (Babylon)), refer to near historical events.

---

[56] C. van Leeuwen, 'The Prophecy of the Yom YHWH in Amos V, 18-20', in *Language and Meaning: Studies in Hebrew Language and Biblical Exegesis*, OTS 19 (Leiden, Brill, 1974), p.130.
[57] G. von Rad, *The Message of the Prophets* (London, SCM Press, 1968), p.99.

This is more difficult to sustain when the 'Day of Yahweh' is applied to *all* nations (Zeph. 3:6-8; Obad. 15; Joel 4:9-14; Zech. 14:1-5). Note also the imagery of cosmic, universal upheaval in Zeph. 1:2-8, that recalls the universal flood of Gen. 7:11-24. In Zeph. 1:2 Yahweh will surely (infinitive absolute plus imperfect) sweep away everything from the face of the earth. Moreover, this will include the destruction of those who complacently accuse him of moral indifference (1:12). In Isa. 2:10-22, the day is against *all* things and *all* people are proud and lofty (2:12-17). It will be a definitive visitation from the LORD:[58] the people hide 'from the glory of his majesty, when he rises to terrify the earth' (2:21).

Thus Cathcart concludes with a distinction between 'a primary day — of intervention by Yahweh with limited effect — and a secondary day — one of universal cosmic judgement'. The 'developed, eschatological Day of Yahweh' may especially be conceded if we grant an 'organic continuity between prophetic preaching and apocalyptic eschatology'.[59] For the latter, we may look to especially to Dan. 12:2, but also note the expectation of a universal judgement of some sort expressed in Eccl. 12:14.

It is therefore not surprising to find the 'Day of Yahweh' being used as the basis for the New Testament proclamation of the day fixed by God 'on which he will have the world judged in righteousness by a man whom he has appointed' (Acts 17:31). With the coming of the Kingdom (Mt. 4:17; Mk. 1:15), the concept of eschatological judgement becomes

---

[58] Ibid., p.95; cf. Williams, 'The Cross and the Punishment of Sin', *op. cit.*, p.88.
[59] K. J. Cathcart, 'Day of Yahweh', *Anchor Bible Dictionary*, vol. 2 (New York, Doubleday, 1992), p.85.

central and unequivocal. The 'day of the Lord' or the 'day of God Almighty' in the New Testament is a future event, of unknown timing; an occasion of great destruction by fire (I Cor. 5:5; I Thess. 5:2; 2 Thess. 2.2; 2 Pet. 3:10, 12; Rev. 16:14). It is the 'day of wrath' (Rom. 2:5; Rev. 6:17), the 'day of Judgement' (Mt. 10:15; 11:22, 24; 12:36; 2 Pet. 2:9; 3:7; I Jn. 4:17). But with Jesus exalted as judge (Jn. 5:22) it is now the 'day of our Lord Jesus Christ' (I Cor. 1:8; 2 Cor. 1:14; Phil. 1:6, 10; 2:16).

Conclusion to section 2: The Character of God and the Purpose of Divine Punishment

We probably accept uncritically the ideas and opinions of our age more than we would care to admit, and this is no doubt especially true of an emotive issue such as punishment. The contemporary understanding of punishment, at least as it is most precisely expressed in the theory of repeated games, sees punishment exclusively as a behavioural concept. We may *talk* of punishment being 'right' or 'just', but underlying this (so the story goes), punishment and the threat of punishment merely serve to sustain a particular pattern of behaviour under the current 'social contract'.

Our investigation of the biblical evidence on divine punishment has confirmed that it may have behavioural intent or effect, especially when it is described as 'discipline' or 'chastisement'. However, the biblical language goes much further than this, and it is difficult to see the language of 'vengeance' as anything other than purely retributive. The first two key examples of divine punishment we have considered, being directed at the resolute stubbornness of Pharaoh and apostate Israel, cannot be described as primarily behavioural. Similarly, warnings about the punishment on the day of eschatological judgement may have secondary behavioural effects, but *at the point of its exercise*, since it involves the complete destruction of the wicked with no suggestion of restoration, its primary purpose must lie elsewhere.

We have considered two major biblical pointers as to the primary purpose of divine punishment. The first comes from the recognition formulae of Exodus and, predominantly in the prophets, Ezekiel. Under contemporary thinking about punishment, the authority to punish comes through social convention. However, the exercise of divine punishment demonstrates the self-legitimating authority of the LORD. The earth is his; other claims to authority are false. The exercise of punishment also reveals that it is by punishing people according to their ways, and for the sake of his name, that he makes himself known. This is related to the second pointer to the purpose of divine punishment: that it is closely linked in the biblical texts to the practical expression of God's hatred of sin.

3.   So is it Necessary for God to Punish Sin?

3.1.   What do we mean by 'necessary'?

We mentioned briefly in the introduction that 'necessity' is generally taken to refer to something that could not have been otherwise. That is, necessity is defined relative to contingency, where a contingent truth is one that is true, but could have been false.

The contemporary discussion of necessity is often couched in the language of 'possible worlds'.[60] So that to say something could not have been otherwise is equivalent to saying that it is true in every possible world: there is no possible world in which it is not true. We shall find this a useful way to think about necessity in what follows.

But what is a 'possible world'? We shall take an epistemic and theistic approach to possible worlds in what follows. That is, worlds are 'possible' from the point of view of an observer with access to that which God reveals about himself in the actual world and predominantly in Scripture. So a world is 'possible' (possibly *actual*), firstly, in the sense that it could be, so far as one can tell, the actual world in which we live. But a world can also be 'possible' (*merely* possible), secondly, in the sense that it is a world that God *could have made* given what we know about his revealed character. We take it that God chose to make a world that is maximally self-glorifying.

---

[60] The seminal contribution is S. Kripke, 'Semantical Considerations on Modal Logic', *Acta Philisophica Fennica*, no. 16, 1963, pp.83-94.

It follows that all possible worlds, on this view, are equally glorifying to God.[61]

On this view, then, possibility and necessity depend upon what God reveals about himself in the actual world and predominantly in Scripture. This gives us an integrative principle, linking the explorations of biblical data in the last section, where we used the methods of biblical studies, with the doctrinal arguments on the necessity of divine punishment considered in this section.

We shall explore three suggested answers to the question in view. First, that it is in no sense necessary for God to punish sin. That is, in at least some possible worlds we can establish clear counter-examples where God does not punish certain sins. Moreover, these counter-examples are not extreme, but rather encompass that (or most of that) which is possibly actual. Secondly, that it is 'hypothetically' necessary for God to punish every sin. This differs from the first answer in that, while there are possible worlds with counter-examples, there is a subset of possible worlds, clearly demarcated (e.g. by a divine decree) and encompassing possibly actual worlds, where God always punishes sin. Thirdly, that it is absolutely necessary for God to punish sin. That is, in every possible world, God punishes every sin.

Now these answers are mutually exclusive, so it would suffice to establish the validity of one to disprove the others — and thereby avoid much repetition of argument.[62] We shall

---

[61] This approach to the metaphysics of possibility will be detailed, God-willing, in a forthcoming paper, 'Divine verses Human Choices', in the *Journal of the Association of Christian Economists*.

[62] Which is one of the features of the *DDJ* — although one cannot but admire

therefore, in Section 3.4 expend most effort establishing the truth of the third answer. Nevertheless, it will be useful heuristically to consider the other answers first at shorter length, at least to clarify the way in which they are then disproved.

3.2.   It is not necessary for God to punish sin

We shall consider three arguments. It is not necessary for God to punish sin: first, if punishment is exclusively behavioural; secondly, if vindicatory justice is opposed to mercy; and thirdly, if we can find any other counter-example suggested by Scripture.

3.2.1.   If punishment is behavioural...

If punishment is exclusively behavioural, as much contemporary discussion would suggest (Section 2.1.2), and God never exercises retributive punishment, then it would not be necessary to punish every sin. In particular, some final and definitive act of punishment would not be necessary. At the point of its exercise it could have no behavioural effect.

We have already seen that the biblical evidence tells strongly against this view. Not only can one establish a strong retributive element to divine punishment (whether looking at the vocabulary of punishment or specific examples — Sections 2.2.1-3), but the biblical account builds up to a climactic act of retributive punishment on the 'day' of Christ's judgement (Section 2.2.4).

Owen's thoroughness!

3.2.2.   If justice is opposed to mercy...

The view that vindicative judgement is opposed to mercy has been most vehemently expressed by Faustus Socinus and his followers. Socinus himself puts it like this:[63] There are two types of divine justice. The first is expressed in God's acts of punishment against the 'wicked and obstinate' and is described in Scripture as 'severity' or 'revenge'. The second is that expressed in the chastisement of the non-obstinate. Moreover, there are two types of mercy: that by which he forgives the repentant, and that by which he draws sinners to himself to make the (conditional) offer of forgiveness. This second type of mercy can also be seen as a form of 'justice', in that it expresses the 'pure and simple kindness of God'. But the first kind of justice is opposed to the first kind of mercy. They cannot be exercised in the 'same time and place' — God does not punish those who turn from their sins. This kind of justice therefore cannot be 'a quality of God', but rather only 'an effect of his will'. It is God's *decision* to punish sin.[64]

To put it another way, we have a counter-example to God's punishment of sin whenever he acts in saving mercy in response to repentance.

In his response to this, John Owen agrees that *at the point of*

---

[63] F. Socinus, *de Jesu Christo Servatore* 1.1, in *Fausti Socini Opera*, vol. 1 (Irenopoli, 1656), pp.122-124. In this account, I am indebted to Garry Williams for access to his notes on the Latin text, which includes translation of the key passages.

[64] Socinus, *de Jesu Christo Servatore* 3.1 — see A. W. Gomes, '*De Jesu Christo Servatore*. Faustus Socinus on the Satisfaction of Christ', *Westminster Theological Journal*, 55, 1993, p.219. Similar sentiments are expressed in the *Racovian Catechism*, translated by T. Rees, (London, Longman, 1818; reprinted Lexington, Kentucky; Amercian Theological Association, 1962), chapter 8, pp.307-308.

exercise justice and mercy are 'different'. But such differences do not mean that the essential principles underlying justice and mercy are contrary. The action of justice, to punish, and the action of mercy, to not punish, would be contrary if applied to the same simple object at the same time. But some divine attributes are not expressed with respect to every work and object, but only to specific objects. Justice is expressed 'by way of habit' towards every sinner; mercy, 'by way of affection', towards some sinners, and for these the justice is expressed by the satisfaction of Christ.[65]

The suggestion that punishment of sin is expressed in the satisfaction of Christ whenever God expresses mercy takes us to the second strand of Socinus' case. This is that in no way can Christ's death be seen as a satisfaction. Rather, it is God's right not to punish sin. Socinus' argument is lengthy, but the heart of it is to present God as a creditor with the absolute right to cancel the debt of our sin without receiving satisfaction.[66] Remission of sins has two parts: that the debtor is freed from obligation, and that the creditor 'does not want satisfaction to be made to himself.'[67] This remains a frequently used argument today. The authors of *The Mystery of Salvation*, for example, claim our 'best theological instincts' lead us to 'personal' analogies to make best sense of the atonement, such as, 'Loving parents will often waive a debt owed to them by a child and they will do all they can to

---

[65] Owen, *DDJ* 8, pp.562-3 (against the Racovian Catechism); also pp.571-4 (against Socinus himself), pp.611-612 (against Rutherford).
[66] Socinus, *de Jesu Christo Servatore* 3.1, pp.186-188. See Gomes, *op. cit.*, pp., 211, 215-6, 222-225. According to Owen's account, a similar view was held by Crellius, Owen, *DDJ* 9, p.567.
[67] Socinus, *de Jesu Christo Servatore* 3.1, p.188.

spare the child the self-destructive effects of its own wrongdoing'.[68]

Returning to Socinus himself, it is interesting that while he is adamant that the redemption language of the Bible is metaphorical, in the sense that there is no actual payment *to* anyone,[69] he does not address the possibility that the debt language might also be metaphorical. The New Testament authors do talk about debt in relation to the atonement, of course, but the sense of being under *economic* obligation (the meaning of *daneion* and one of the meanings of *ophilēma*) only really comes across in a handful of metaphors or parables.[70] That is, the biblical data never suggests that the atonement actually *is* the honouring of an exchange or the canceling of a debt contract. The focus in the debt or redemption metaphors seems to be on the divine cost in providing atonement, and on the liberating effects of atonement — comparable to a release from slavery or debt. In other words, Socinus is over-stretching a biblical metaphor to make his case[71] (a similar criticism could be made, of course, of Anselm[72]). When we consider the more literal biblical

---

[68] *The Mystery of Salvation, op. cit.*, p.212.
[69] Socinus, *de Jesu Christo Servatore* 2.1 – 2.2, pp.140-143. See Gomes, *op. cit.*, pp.220-222.
[70] Mt. 18: 23-35; Lk. 7:40-43; Rom. 4:4.
[71] Owen, *DDJ* 9, p.567; also Grotius *De Satisfactione Christi* (hereafter *DSC*), in *Hugo Grotius Opera Theologica* I, ed. E. Rabbie, tr. H. Mulder (Assen/Maastricht, Van Gorcum, 1990), 2.15, pp.141-143; cf. Williams, *A Critical Exposition..., op.cit.*, pp.21-22, 35. In his discussion of Socinus' treatment of redemption language (*DSC* 8.8-19, pp.229-235), Grotius would have done better by talking of a literal *cost* in the atonement rather than a literal price, since, strictly speaking, a price is a rate of exchange between two parties.
[72] Anselm, *Cur Deus Homo*, esp. 1.10, 1.11, 1.15, in (e.g.) *Monologion, Proslogion, Cur Deus Homo* and *De Conceptu Virginali*, in *Anselm of Canterbury*, edited and

descriptions of sin as rebellion and law-breaking it is no longer at all obvious that God can simply ignore it, as we shall see in Section 3.3.

Both Owen and Grotius make the case that the atonement is indeed concerned with the *satisfaction* of divine justice, rather than the putting aside of that justice, from Rom. 3:21-26.[73] The atonement was, says Paul, *eis* (3:25) or *pros tēn* (3:26) 'an evidence of his righteousness' (3:25, 26). We shall return to this idea of *evidencing* God's justice in 3.3.4.

3.2.3. *If we can find any other counter-example suggested by Scripture...*

To test the claim that the exercise of vindicatory punishment is not necessary, we have been looking for a counter-example: a clear example of God permanently deciding not to punish a given sin. If a counter-example is not suggested by the purpose of punishment being behavioural, or by the exercise of God's mercy, then could there be some other counter-example?

One cannot deny a great deal of withdrawal and mitigation of punishment in the biblical accounts. However, the task of establishing any of these as clear counter-examples is far from straightforward. Many are examples of acts of mercy towards God's covenant people — an apparent counter-example we have already considered. Other apparent counter-examples can always be understood as a change of degree or

---

translated by J. Hopkins and H. Richardson (Toronto and New York, The Edwin Mellen Press, 1976).
[73] Owen, *DDJ* 5, pp.546-549; 10, p.572. Grotius, *DSC* 1.41, p.117; cf. Williams, *A Critical Exposition...*, op. cit., pp.51-53.

timing of punishment,[74] especially given the biblical evidence for a final cosmic judgement (section 2.2.4). Recall also the non-straightforward administration of punishment in the Genesis account (Section 2.2).

Covering the punishment of every sin by either the cross or a final eschatological judgement in this way might seem to be too good to be true, rendering the claim that God punishes every sin unfalsifiable. This might be a fair criticism if the links between sins and these acts of punishment were not made in Scripture. However, Rom. 3:21-26 (cf. Heb. 9:15) links the punishment of the sins of God's covenant people to the cross, and in, for example, Eccl. 12:14 it is clear that God will bring *every* deed to judgement, including every hidden thing.

3.3. It is hypothetically necessary for God to punish sin

The intermediate position, that God punishes sin with an hypothetical necessity, is summarised by Owen thus:

> God hath decreed to let no sin pass unpunished without a satisfaction; [and] that decree being supposed... [only then could one say] that a satisfaction was necessary.[75]

However, there does seem to be some variation in the particular views held by proponents of hypothetical necessity.

For example, according to Owen's account, William Twisse held that sin-avenging justice is an essential attribute of the divine nature, but claimed that God could forgive sin without

---

[74] Owen, *DDJ* 2, p.509; cf. F. Turretin, *Institutes of Elenctic Theology* (hereafter *IET*), 3 vols., translated by G. M. Giger and edited by J. T. Dennison Jr. (Phillipsburg, P&R Publishing, 1992), 3.19.4 and 3.19.23.
[75] Owen, *DDJ* 2, p.507.

a satisfaction[76] (presumably, apart from his decree). In response, Owen is simply and understandably baffled. Owen's other Reformed opponent in the *DDJ*, Samuel Rutherford, is more consistent when he maintains that 'punitory justice exists not in God by necessity of nature, but freely'.[77]

There is certainly plenty of scope for confusion in these accounts, and it may be that the debate was clouded by differences concerning how the attributes of God relate to external acts. For example, both Twisse and Rutherford seem to think that to describe the exercise of vindicatory justice as necessary would unduly restrict the freedom of God. All parties agree a particular freedom in God's decision to create,[78] but Rutherford seems to want to extend an identical freedom to God's actions in the world. So: God could have decided not to create; God could have decided not to decree punishment for sin.

Owen's response was to say that divine attributes with an external object, such as vindicatory justice, are compatible with 'concomitant liberty' in their exercise, but not with 'antecedent indifference'.[79] This is obscure language, to say the least. What did Owen mean? Just that the necessity we are talking about is not the 'absolute necessity of nature, as

---

[76] Owen, *DDJ* 12, p.585.

[77] Owen, *DDJ* 18, p.608; cf. 2, p.507.

[78] As Rutherford says, 'he might, if so it had pleased him, never have intended to shew forth his own Glory... he might never have created the world... For he was sufficient within himself', S. Rutherford, *The Covenant of Life Opened; or A Treatise of the Covenant of Grace* 7.3 (Edinburgh, Robert Brown, 1655; facsimile proved by Still Waters Revival Books, Edmonton, Canada), p.31; cf. Acts 17:25.

[79] Owen *DDJ* 13, p.589; cf. Turretin, *IET* 3.19.5.

the Father begets the Son'[80] – which would indeed conflict with God's 'antecedent indifference'. The necessity we are dealing with is that which is necessary for God's self-glorification, *given* the decision to create. How does the hypothetical view fare in this setting?

On the one hand, one can easily concur that given the decree, God will certainly keep it. There seems to be broad consensus on this point, which can be traced back at least to Athanasius.[81] The argument is expressed with particular cogency by Jonathan Edwards, who explains:

> ...from the truth of God there is an inviolable connection between absolute threatenings and execution, not so properly from an obligation on God to conform the execution to the past absolute threatenings, as on his obligation to conform his absolute threatenings to the future execution. This God was absolutely obliged to do, as he would speak the truth.[82]

On the other hand, the hypothetical view maintains that there exist possible worlds where there is no decree to punish sin. Rutherford states explicitly that the decree to punish sin must be contingent. He argues this by asking whether, had the decree not been made, 'should he have lost his natural dominion over men in that case?'[83] But the approach to possible worlds we have adopted here (see above) tells us that if possible worlds exist in which God does not decree punishment for sin, they must be equally glorifying to him as

---

[80] Ibid.

[81] Athanasius, *On the Incarnation of the Word* 6, 7.

[82] J. Edwards, 'Miscellanies 779: The Necessity of Satisfaction for Sin' (hereafter *NSS*), in *The Miscellanies 501-832*, vol. 18 of *The Works of Jonathan Edwards*, edited by A. Chamberlain (New Haven and London, Yale University Press, 2000), p.445.

[83] Rutherford, *op. cit.*, p.26.

those that do. We shall return to whether God could be so indifferent to the role of Law-giver in Section 3.4.4 below.

3.4.   It is absolutely necessary for God to punish sin

We shall consider five principal lines of argument: from intuition, from maximal mercy, from God's hatred of sin, from the demonstrative nature of divine punishment, and from the death of Christ.

3.4.1.   The argument from intuition

Turretin[84] argues that the rightness of the exercise of punishment of sin is confirmed by both conscience and the 'consent of the people'.[85]

Edwards has a more extended argument.[86] He begins: 'None will deny but that some crimes are so horrid and so deserving of punishment, that 'tis requisite that they should not go unpunished'. (He might have added: even Socinus would not deny this.) Moreover, none would deny that there should be some proportionality in the punishment, such that 'great crimes should be punished with punishment in some measure answerable to the heinousness of the crime'. However, deeper reflection shows that *any* crime is a sin against God, and any sin against God is 'infinitely heinous'. Therefore, he concludes, 'by what was before granted, 'tis requisite that God should punish it'.

This is fine so far as it goes. The difficulty of course is that for

---

[84] Condensing Owen without acknowledgement!
[85] Turretin, *IET* 3.19.8, p.238; cf. Owen, *DDJ* 3.2 and 4, pp.522-541.
[86] Edwards, *NSS* I, pp.434-437.

someone whose conscience does not point this way, or within a society with no such consensus, the argument is less persuasive.

3.4.2. *The argument from maximal mercy*

Owen's earlier view on necessity in the *Death of Death in the Death of Christ* (1647) was that it was the decree to make satisfaction by God's Son that made the exercise of vindicative justice necessary, and nothing antecedent to that. This decree was so that 'he would manifest his glory'.[87] He was perhaps borrowing from Augustine, who says that while other means of salvation were open to God, 'there neither was nor need have been any other mode more appropriate for curing our misery'.[88] Calvin makes a passing remark along similar lines in his commentary on John: 'God could have redeemed us by a word or a wish, but another way seemed better to him for our benefit: that, not sparing his own much-loved Son, he might testify in his person how much he cares for our salvation'.[89]

This is sometimes described as an 'hypothetical' view,[90] and its proponents suggest that they thought of it this way themselves when they say that the decree could have been otherwise. But, on the view of possible worlds and necessity

---

[87] J. Owen, 'The Death of Death in the Death of Christ', in W. H. Goold (ed.) *The Works of John Owen*, volume 10, (London, Johnstone & Hunter, 1850-55), chapter 2, p.205.
[88] Augustine, *De Trinitate* xiii.13.
[89] J. Calvin, *The Gospel According to St. John 11-21 and the First Epistle of John*, Calvin's Commentaries, trans. T. H. L. Parker, ed. D. W. Torrance and T. F. Torrance (Edinburgh, Saint Andrew Press, 1961), p.100.
[90] e.g. J. Murray, *Redemption Accomplished and Applied* (Edinburgh, Banner of Truth Trust, 1979; first published Grand Rapids, Eerdmans, 1961), pp.11-12.

we are taking, the decree could *not* have been otherwise if (as suggested) it was essential for the self-glorification of God. Moreover, if the exercise of vindicatory judgement is necessary for the making of satisfaction by the death of Christ, and the latter is necessary for God's self-glorification, then the exercise of vindicatory judgement is also necessary for God's glorification. This is therefore best seen as an argument for absolute necessity.

However, it is not an especially persuasive one.[91] It is difficult to think of any direct Scriptural support and, at least on its own, it does suggest a certain indifference to sin in itself on behalf of God. There are better ways of arguing from the death of Christ, as we shall see below (Section 3.4.5).

3.4.3.   The argument from expression of hatred of sin

Perhaps the simplest and most persuasive argument in favour of the necessary exercise of sin-punishing justice is to begin with God's hatred of sin. We have already considered the very strong biblical evidence in favour of God's hatred of sin (Section 2.2), and these are so strong and seem so related to his essential being (rather than his decretive will)[92] that it seems quite reasonable to assert that God hates sin in every possible world — it is essential to his self-glorification.

But what, says Owen, is hating sin apart from willing to

---

[91] Ibid., pp.12-18.
[92] Carl Trueman argues that it was in finding this 'epistemological pathway from God's revelation to his essence' that Owen changed his views on the necessary exercise of punishment — C. R. Trueman, 'John Owen's *Dissertation on Divine Justice*: An Exercise in Christocentric Scholasticism', *Calvin Theological Journal*, 33 (1998), pp.98-102.

punish it?[93] Owen points especially to the metaphor of God hating sin as a consuming fire (Heb. 12:29, quoting Deut 4:24; Isa. 4:24; 23:14; Jer. 44:4),[94] and to Psalm 5:5-6 [Eng], where hatred of sin and destruction of the sinner are tied close together.[95] If he *wants* to punish sin, and is able to do so, can it be supposed that he will endure eternally the displeasure of not doing so?[96]

Edwards puts the claim very plainly: 'If God's nature be infinitely opposite to sin, then doubtless he has a disposition answerable to oppose it in his acts and works... God, by his necessary infinite hatred of sin, is necessarily disposed to punish it with a punishment answerable to his hatred'.[97]

We saw much in Section 2 to reinforce this view. There is a strong lexical connection between God's anger at sin and his expression of that anger in punishment (2.2.1.1). This is particularly striking in the warnings of the destruction of Jerusalem (2.2.3). Indeed, the connection is so strong that words for sin are sometimes used as metonyms for punishment (2.2.1.2). Moreover, the characteristic of 'by no means' leaving sin unpunished is intrinsic to the name of the LORD (2.2.2).

So the argument here is very simple. We claim that the biblical evidence on the nature of God's hatred of sin means

---

[93] Owen, *DDJ* 6.1, p.550.

[94] Owen, *DDJ* 6.2, p.553. Owen might have added Num. 11:1; Ps 59:13; Isa. 10:17, 30:27; Lam 2:3; Ezek. 22:31; Zeph. 1:18, amongst other references. Hab. 1:13 is also a clear expression of God's essential intolerance of sin (the implication is: he will not fail to deal with it).

[95] Owen, *DDJ* 6.1, p.550.

[96] Owen, *DDJ* 6.1, p.552; cf. Turretin, *IET* 3.19.11, p.237.

[97] Edwards, *NSS* 2, pp.437-8.

that it strictly implies (or entails) the punishment of sin. So,

[Argument 1]

(1)   God necessarily hates every sin.

(2)   God's hatred of each sin strictly implies his punishment of that sin.

(3)   Therefore God necessarily punishes every sin.

3.4.4.   *Arguments from the demonstrative nature of divine punishment*

We have already seen how punishment of sin is a straightforward *expression* of God's holiness and his hatred of sin, but of course it also *demonstrates* his holiness and hatred of sin. So Owen argues that it demonstrates his justice, his holiness and his natural dominion.[98] Or rather it preserves 'his glory entire to all eternity'[99] in these three areas — which is equivalent to saying that the demonstrative effect of punishing sin is essential to his self-glorification.

The three characteristics demonstrated by divine punishment are closely related, of course. For example, the decree to punish sin in Gen. 2:17 and expressed in the Law is an expression of God's holiness and dominion. So Edwards talks about the Law as an 'expression of the perfection of the Lawgiver'.[100] Indeed, the Law is given in a context that

---

[98] Owen, *DDJ* 7, pp.554-556;11, pp.581-2;13, p.587.

[99] Owen, *DDJ* 7, p.554.

[100] Edwards, *NSS* 4, p.443. Similarly, Grotius is keen to point out that God is not a judge under the Law, but rather a Ruler expressing his ontological goodness through his rule and hence through the Law (H. Grotius, *Meletius*, critical edition with translation, commentary and introduction by G. H. M. Posthumus Meyjes (Leiden, Brill, 1988; first published 1611), 8, p.106).

emphasises, with great acts of power and with direct declarations, the dominion and holiness of God.[101] If punishing every sin demonstrates God's holiness (i.e. his hatred of sin), then it simultaneously demonstrates that he judges rightly according to the Law.

However, how do we argue from the demonstrative nature of divine punishment to the necessity of exercising it?

Recall from our discussion of the biblical data the importance of the recognition formulae in establishing the purpose of divine punishment (Sections 2.2.2 and 2.2.3). These not only show us that divine punishment has a demonstrative element, but also give us the context in which the demonstration takes place. It is a context of extensive false belief: the Egyptians worshipping an array of false Gods; the Israelites turning to idols. It is a context of 'epistemological smearing' — '...their senseless minds were darkened', as Paul puts it (Rom. 1:21). *Ex ante*, prior to the demonstrative act of punishment, many would have been questioning the character of God — his 'name' would not have been known. In such a context, the non-punishment of a given sin would leave open the possibility that God's hatred of sin does not extend so far as that sin. Even if God *said* he hated it, darkened, unbelieving minds would not be forced to acknowledge his hatred until he demonstrated it.[102] Extending the logic of Rom. 3:21-26, for example, can we really suggest

---

[101] Thus the keynote phrases in Leviticus 17-26 are 'I am the LORD' (repeated many, many times), 'I am the LORD your God', and 'I am the LORD your God; sanctify yourselves therefore, and be holy, for I am holy' (19:2; 20:7-8, 22-26).
[102] cf. Edwards, who points out that if there had been only a declaration of God's hatred of sin, 'the creature might have believed it, but could not have seen it, unless [God] should also take vengeance for it' (Edwards, *NSS* 2, p.439).

that if God acted in punishment against his Son to remove one set of apparent counter-examples to his divine justice, he would leave any other counter-examples?

This suggests the following proposition:

(4)   Non-punishment of sin implies that God has not demonstrated his hatred of sin.

We can argue that (4) must be true in every possible world — because the existence of sin and darkened minds in the actual world are no surprise to God, but rather exist under the sovereignty of God to his glory.[103] This adaptation gives us the following argument:

[Argument 2]

(4)'   Non-punishment of sin *strictly* implies that God has not demonstrated his hatred of sin.

(5)   God necessarily demonstrates his hatred of sin.

(6)   Therefore, God necessarily punishes every sin.

Owen's argument that punishment of sin is necessary to demonstrate God's dominion is less obvious. Owen claims that the structure of the Creator-creature relation is restored by punishment.[104] However, it is not quite clear how punishment restores the relation, or whether there might be other means by which the relation could be restored (e.g. by

---

[103] Those unhappy with this can look ahead to Argument 4 in the next section, where we demonstrate the necessity of the death of Christ. If sin and darkened minds are not necessary, then the death of Christ would not be necessary.

[104] Owen *DDJ* 2, p.551; 11, pp.581-2; 13, p.587. Anselm makes a similar point when he claims that in punishment the sinner 'becomes subservient, under infinite wisdom, to the order and beauty of the universe', *Cur Deus Homo* 1.15

repentance alone).

Given the stress we have seen in the recognition formulae on demonstrating the dominion of God (e.g. in Exod. 9:29, '...so that you may know that the earth is the LORD's'), it would be good to rescue Owen's argument. Owen himself hints at a possible solution towards the end of his *Dissertation*, when he describes sin against God as that 'which earnestly wishes him *not to be God*[105] (cf. Rom. 8:7). That is, every sinner effectively utters the blasphemous lie 'you are not LORD'; every unpunished sinful act stands as a declaration against God's dominion. This suggests the following variation on Argument 2:

[Argument 3]

(7)   Non-punishment of sin strictly implies that God has not demonstrated his dominion (by countering the false declaration that he is not LORD).

(8)   God necessarily demonstrates his dominion.

(9)   Therefore, God necessarily punishes every sin.

3.4.5.   The Christological argument

The final argument we shall consider is Owen's Christological argument:

> Were the opinions of the adversaries to be admitted, and were we to suppose that God might will the salvation of any sinner, it will be difficult, if not impossible, to assign any sufficient and necessary cause of the death of Christ... *[if sins were easily remissible]*... what sufficient reason could be given, pray, then, why he should lay those sins, so easily remissible, to the charge

---

[105] Owen, *DDJ* 18, p.619.

of his most holy Son, and on their account subject him to such dreadful sufferings?[106]

Notice first that Owen takes it as self-evident that 'the salvation of any sinner' is accomplished by God laying their sins 'to the charge of his most holy Son'. That is, Christ died a sin-bearing death on behalf of forgiven sinners.[107] Owen then argues that if it were possible for a forgiven sinner to exist without their sin being (eventually) punished, then it is inconceivable that Christ would have been sent to die a sin-bearing death.

A formal version of Owen's argument in the language of possible worlds might go as follows:

[Argument 4]

Owen takes it as self-evident that Christ died a sin-bearing death on behalf of forgiven sinners. That is, we assert:

(10)   In the actual world, Christ died a sin-bearing death on behalf of forgiven sinners.

We can express Owen's belief in the incompatibility of easily remissible sins with the sin-bearing death of Christ by asserting:

(11)   In every possible world, if a forgiven sinner exists without their sin being punished, then Christ does not die a sin-bearing death in that world.

Now recall that given the way we are thinking about possible

---

[106] Owen, *DDJ* 7.4, p.556; cf. Turretin *IET* 3.19.15, p.239.
[107] For a thorough contemporary defence of this claim see D. Peterson, *op. cit.*; also see, on the language of sin-bearing applied to the death of Christ (e.g. 1 Peter 2:24-5), G. Williams, 'The Cross and the Punishment of Sin' *op. cit.* One can also argue from the death of Christ itself, since death is the penalty for sin (Gen 2:17).

worlds (outlined above), a world is only 'possible' if we can rightly conceive of God creating it in place of the actual world. And we can only rightly conceive of him doing so if it would have been equally glorifying to him. But suppose there is a 'merely' possible world in which (10) is not true. This seems horribly contradictory: given the cost of giving his Son over to death, how could God have chosen an actual world where his Son does die a sin-bearing death on behalf of forgiven sinners, when he could have chosen an 'equally glorifying' world in which he does not? We conclude:

(12)   In *every* possible world, Christ died a sin-bearing death on behalf of forgiven sinners.

This suggests, then, that there does not exist a possible world in which forgiven sinners can exist without their sin being punished. That is, (11) and (12) lead to the conclusion:[108]

(13)   Therefore, in every possible world, forgiven sinners are punished for their sin (punished in Christ).

One more step is needed to seal the case. That is to say, there is nothing special about forgiven sinners that makes their sin more punishable than anyone else's!

(14)   If forgiven sinners are punished for their sin, then *all* sinners are punished for their sin.

From (13) and (14) it then follows,

(15)   Therefore, it is absolutely necessary that sinners be punished for their sin.

The Christological argument, by proceeding from the central

---

[108] In terms of modal logic, this argument has a very similar structure to Arguments 2 and 3.

truth of the Christian faith, which is the death of Christ, gives us what is probably the most compelling case that divine justice is *certain*. What's more, divine justice is *essential* to God, and worthy of praise.

4. Conclusion

From the biblical data on divine punishment we have seen that divine punishment is more than behavioural, that it expresses God's hatred of sin, and that God uses it to make himself known. This has led us to three principal (logically valid) lines of argument that God necessarily punishes every sin. He does so first as an expression of his holiness; secondly, as a demonstration of his holiness, justice and dominion; and thirdly, we know that the punishment of every sin is necessary from the death of his Son.

The most obvious implication of the necessity of God punishing every sin is the necessity of Christ's satisfaction. As Turretin puts it, the necessary exercise of God's justice 'necessarily demands the infliction of punishment either on the sinner himself or on the surety substituted in his place'.[109] We have not had the opportunity here to address the full range of objections to the penal doctrine of the atonement. However, if the first two principal arguments[110] we have made are sound and valid, then it seems there would be very little hope of salvation if the penal doctrine were false. We are thus led to an understanding of the atonement very different from those briefly outlined in the introduction. In the Church of England, this should be an encouragement to 'expound and

---

[109] Turretin, *IES* 14.10.17; vol.2, p.422.
[110] That God necessarily punishes every sin as an *expression* of his holiness and as a *demonstration* of his holiness, justice and dominion. The Christological argument works the other way: given that the death of Christ is penal and necessary, we know that the punishment of every sin is necessary.

teach' the doctrine of the atonement 'as the Church of England has received it'[111] and as it is expressed in the *39 Articles*.

We shall briefly consider some further areas of application.

The first follows from the relation between necessity, as we have understood it here, and the glorification of God. If the divine punishment of every sin is necessary, then it is a worthy subject for doxology. It does not take much reflection, however, to note how little mention the doctrine of divine punishment gets in the practice of the church today. Even in gospel presentations, it is sometimes glossed over with some sense of embarrassment. It is hardly a major feature of our singing (apart from Psalmody of course!). We need to ask ourselves whether we could comfortably join in the hymn of Rev. 19:1-3.

The second comes from the distinction between statements *de dicto* (i.e. statements about propositions) and statements *de re* (about the properties of certain things). One can prove that if God necessarily punishes every sin, then sin has *the necessary property of being punished by God*. This may not seem very striking at first, and the *de dicto – de re* distinction is disputed,[112] but putting it this way does emphasise the fearful seriousness of sin.

Thirdly, there are implications for our evangelism: not only for the *urgency* of evangelism, given that people outside Christ will personally bear inevitable divine punishment, but

---

[111] See the vows made in The Ordination of Priests (also called Presbyters), in The Alternative Service Book 1980 (St. Ives, SPCK, 1980), p.358.
[112] R. Girle, Modal Logics and Philosophy, (Teddington, Acumen, 2000), p.119.

we must also conclude that unless we *tell* people God must punish their sins, *and why*, we have failed to tell them the full story. We bring glory to God when we proclaim his majesty and goodness and justice.

Fourthly, there is the motivation to love. John's agenda in reminding us of Jesus' death (1 John 4:7-12) is to encourage genuine love between believers. John wants us to know and understand God's love for us better and better, and he wants us to behave accordingly, as God's children. As we love our brothers and sisters in Christ, he wants us to have that deep assurance that we are indeed children of God. But to know all that, we also need to know that apart from Christ we deserve to die. That either we die or he dies on our behalf, demonstrating God's justice and majesty, expressing his hatred of sin. The more we understand and experience that, John tells us, the more we will understand God's love, and the more able we are to express true love ourselves.

Finally, as we consider this sober doctrine, let us dwell deeply on God's love for us. We live in a world yearning deeply for genuine love. The person who trusts Jesus and is convinced of God's justice then has access to the most precious thing in the world. It's at the heart of a strong relationship with our Heavenly Father. It's *the* definitive expression of love, and it's ours to experience and enjoy.

Bibliography

Primary Sources

Anselm, *Cur Deus Homo*, in (e.g.) *Monologion, Proslogion, Cur Deus Homo* and *De Conceptu Virginali*, in *Anselm of Canterbury*, edited and translated by Jasper Hopkins and Herbert Richardson (Toronto and New York, The Edwin Mellen Press, 1976).

Athanasius, On the Incarnation of the Word.

Calvin, J., *The Gospel According to St. John 11-21 and the First Epistle of John*, Calvin's Commentaries, trans. T. H. L. Parker, ed. D. W. Torrance and T. F. Torrance (Edinburgh, Saint Andrew Press, 1961).

Edwards, J., *Freedom of the Will*, edited by P. Ramsey, (New Haven and London, Yale University Press, 1957; first published 1754).

— 'Miscellanies 779: The Necessity of Satisfaction for Sin', in *The Miscellanies 501-832*, vol. 18 of *The Works of Jonathan Edwards*, edited by A. Chamberlain (New Haven and London, Yale University Press, 2000), pp.434-448.

Grotius, H., *Meletius*, critical edition with translation, commentary and introduction by G. H. M. Posthumus Meyjes (Leiden, Brill, 1988; first published 1611).

— *De Satisfactione Christi*, in *Hugo Grotius Opera Theologica* I, ed. E. Rabbie, tr. H. Mulder (Assen/Maastricht, Van Gorcum, 1990).

Owen, J., 'The Death of Death in the Death of Christ', in W. H. Goold (ed.) *The Works of John Owen*, volume 10, (London, Johnstone & Hunter, 1850-55), pp.139-479.

— *A Dissertation on Divine Justice* (Oxford, Thomas Robinson, 1653), in W. H. Goold (ed.) *The Works of John Owen*, vol. 10 (London, Johnstone & Hunter, 1850-55), pp.481-624.

The Racovian Catechism, translated by T. Rees, (London, Longman, 1818; reprinted Lexington, Kentucky; Amercian Theological Association, 1962).

Rutherford, S., *The Covenant of Life Opened; or A Treatise of the Covenant of Grace* 7.3 (Edinburgh, Robert Brown, 1655; facsimile provided by Still Waters Revival Books, Edmonton, Canada).

Socinus, de Jesu Christo Servatore, in Fausti Socini Opera, vol. 1 (Irenopoli, 1656).

Turretin, F., *Institutes of Elenctic Theology*, 3 vols., translated by G. M. Giger and edited by J. T. Dennison Jr. (Phillipsburg, P&R Publishing, 1992).

Secondary Sources

Axelrod, R., *The Evolution of Cooperation*, (Harmondsworth, Penguin Books, 1990).

Baloian, B., 'Anger', *NIDOTTE* vol.4, pp.377-385.

Barr, J., The Semantics of Biblical Language (Oxford, OUP, 1961).

Binmore, K., *Game Theory and the Social Contract* Volume I, *Playing Fair*, (Cambridge MA, MIT Press, 1994); Volume II, *Just Playing*, (Cambridge MA, MIT Press, 1998).

Blocher, H., In the Beginning: The Opening Chapters of Genesis (Leicester, IVP, 1984).

Cathcart, K. J., 'Day of Yahweh', *Anchor Bible Dictionary*, vol. 2 (New York, Doubleday, 1992), pp.84-85.

Chalke, S., and A. Mann, *The Lost Message of Jesus* (Grand Rapids, Zondervan, 2004).

Cooper, B., *Just Love: Why God Must Punish Sin* (New Malden, The Good Book Company, 2005).

Eichrodt, W., *Theology of the Old Testament*, vol. 1 (London, SCM, 1961).

Enns, P., *Exodus*, NIV Application Commentary (Grand Rapids, Michigan; Zondervan, 2000).

Fiddes, P., *Past Event and Present Salvation* (London; Darton, Longman & Todd, 1989).

Fudenberg, D., and J. Tirole, *Game Theory*, (Cambrindge, Mass; MIT Press, 1991).

Girle, R., *Modal Logics and Philosophy*, (Teddington, Acumen, 2000).

Gomes, A. W. '*De Jesu Christo Servatore*: Faustus Socinus on the Satisfaction of Christ', *Westminster Theological Journal*, 55, 1993, pp.209-231.

Herion, G., 'Wrath of God (OT)', *Anchor Bible Dictionary*, vol. 6 (New York, Doubleday, 1992).

Kittel, G. and G. Friedrich (eds.), *Theological Dictionary of the New Testament* (TDNT), 10 vols., trans. G. W. Bromiley (Grand Rapids, Eerdmans, 1977).

Krašovek, J., Reward, Punishment and Forgiveness: The Thinking and Beliefs of Ancient Israel in the Light of Greek and Modern Views, VT sup. 78 (Leiden, Brill, 1999).

Kreps, *A Course in Microeconomic Theory* (New York, Harvester Wheatsheaf, 1990).

Kripke, S., 'Semantical Considerations on Modal Logic', *Acta Philisophica Fennica*, no. 16, 1963, pp.83-94.

Luc, A. 'חטא', *NIDOTTE* vol.2, pp.87-93.

Mertens, J.-F., 'Supergames', in *The New Palgrave: Game Theory*, edited by J. Eatwell, M. Milgate and P. Newman (London, Macmillan, 1987), pp.238-241.

Murray, J., *Redemption Accomplished and Applied* (Edinburgh, Banner of Truth Trust, 1979; first published Grand Rapids, Eerdmans, 1961).

The Mystery of Salvation: The Story of God's Gift, a Report by the Doctrine Commission of the General Synod of the Church of England (London, Church House Publishing, 1995).

O'Donovan, O. and R. J. Song, 'Punishment' in *The New Dictionary of Theology*, ed. S. B. Ferguson and D. F. Wright (Leicester, IVP, 1988), pp.547-549.

Olivier, J. P. J., 'נקה', *NIDOTTE*, vol. 3, pp.152-153.

Osborne, M. J. and A. Rubinstein, *A Course in Game Theory*, (Cambridge, Mass.; MIT Press, 1994).

Ovey, M., 'The Cross, Creation and the Human Predicament', in David Peterson (ed.), *Where Wrath and Mercy Meet*, (Carlisle, Paternoster, 2001).

Peels, H. G. L., 'נקם', *NIDOTTE* vol. 3

Peterson, D., 'Atonement in the New Testament' in D. Peterson (ed.) *Where Wrath and Mercy Meet*, (Carlisle, Paternoster, 2001), pp.26-67.

Trueman, C. R., 'John Owen's *Dissertation on Divine Justice:* An Exercise in Christocentric Scholasticism', *Calvin Theological Journal*, 33 (1998), pp.87-103.

VanGemeren, W. A. (ed.), *New International Dictionary of Old Testament Theology and Exegesis* (NIDOTTE), 5 vols. (Carlise, Paternoster, 1997).

van Leeuwen, C., 'The Prophecy of the Yom YHWH in Amos V, 18-20', in *Language and Meaning: Studies in Hebrew Language and Biblical Exegesis*, OTS 19 (Leiden, Brill, 1974), pp.113-134.

von Neumann, J. and O. Morgenstern, *Theory of Games and Economic Behaviour* (Princeton, Princeton University Press, 1947).

von Rad, G., *The Message of the Prophets* (London, SCM Press, 1968).

Waltke, B. K., *Genesis: A Commentary*, (Grand-Rapids, Michigan; Zondervan, 2001).

Wenham, G. J., *Genesis 1-15*, WBC (Waco, Texas; Word Books, 1987).

Williams, G., 'The Cross and the Punishment of Sin', in D. Peterson (ed.), *Where Wrath and Mercy Meet: Proclaiming the Atonement Today*, (Carlisle, Paternoster, 2001), pp.68-99.

— A Critical Exposition of Hugo Grotius's Doctrine of the Atonement in De satisfactione Christi, unpublished D.Phil. thesis (Oxford, 1999).

Zimmerli, W., 'I am Yaweh' (first published 1954), reprinted in Zimmerli, W., *I am Yahweh*, trans. D. W. Stott (Atlanta, John Knox Press, 1982), pp.1-28;

— 'Knowledge of God According to the Book of Ezekiel' (first published 1954), reprinted in Zimmerli, *I am Yahweh*, trans. D. W. Stott (Atlanta, John Knox Press, 1982), pp.29-98.